THE INTERSECTION OF BEAUTY AND CRIME

poems by

Jawanza Phoenix

First Edition

ISBN: 1453725954

EAN-13: 9781453725955

cover art by Elvis Perez

author photo by Karen Douglas

Acknowledgments

Many thanks to the following people who read and commented on earlier versions of this work: Erin Shea Fleming, Gail Fishman Gerwin, Dale Muto, Frances Lombardi-Grahl, Howard Berelson, Lisa Dahlborg, Traci Probst, Susan Lembo Balik, Christine Redman Waldeyer, Laura McCullough, Ginger Williams, Patricia Hanahoe-Dosch, Flower Conroy, Mariahadessa Ekere Tallie, and Willie Perdomo.

Many thanks to Maria Mazziotti Gillan and Laura Boss, organizers of the writer's retreat held at the Convent of Saint John the Baptist, Saint Marguerite's Retreat House in Mendham, New Jersey.

Many thanks to Peter E. Murphy, organizer of the writer's retreat held at the Grand Hotel in Cape May, New Jersey.

Many thanks to Mark Brunetti and Anthony Buccino for numerous insights on self-publishing.

Many thanks to all others who helped me on this journey.

for my mother

and my clients

CONTENTS

Questions

Portraits

Letters

Revelations

Prayers

QUESTIONS

How Can You Defend Him If You Know He is Guilty?

because I never know, just like I never know if what TV tells me
about the war in Iraq is the truth
because I wasn't there when it happened
because cops lie and plant evidence
because cops are not allowed to break the law in order to catch
those who they believe are breaking the law
because guilt or innocence doesn't matter in court,
only what can be proven
because most so-called evidence is like a house of cards,
ready to collapse at any time
because mistaken eyewitness identification is the single greatest
cause of wrongful convictions
because Blacks and Latinos were not designed
to commit crimes
because evidence like shiny red apples
might have worms lurking inside
because evidence like luscious green grass
might have ticks with Lyme disease
because evidence like waves on white sand beaches
might have unseen rip currents
because dogs are your best friends until they mangle you
from head to toe
because nobody believed women when they said their husbands
were beating them behind closed doors
because nobody believed Native Americans when they said their
ancestors were buried under corporate buildings
because generations of Black and Latino men have been
beaten down and broken by the system
because he does not look much different than me

because what if he was me and *I swear I didn't do it*
and I only told 'em I did it cuz they starved me and beat me
and I wudda said anything to stop the abuse
and I been good my whole life
and I just wanna go home to my kids
and I thought cops were supposed to be good
and not rotten like human shit in a bottle

How Can You Let Him Plead Guilty If You Know He is Innocent?

because nothing beats the sweet taste of
    freedom now
    freedom now
    freedom now
because when people are drowning and think they're about to die
    and they don't want to die,
    they will do anything
because predominantly white juries usually do not presume
    innocence before proof of guilt when
    the accused is black, noticeably Latino or visibly Muslim,
    forcing him to prove his innocence
because when he has no witnesses, videotapes or audiotapes to
    vouch for his story,
    he has no proof
because just like innocent lambs are often sacrificed to
    obtain favors from God,
    the accused can sacrifice himself to
    get Time Served
because what if he was me and *I swear I didn't do it*
    but I miss my wife and kids who I haven't seen in over a year
    and I'm tired of waiting for trial and living here where
    people fight over stupid shit everyday
    and I eat the same greasy slime everyday
    and I cannot feel the sun or the wind on my skin

How Can A Criminal Actually Be Good?

Jerome's son knows his father from playing catch with footballs and playing chess. The streets know him for his adeptness at stealing cars.

Muhammad whose checkered past scares companies into saying, *no thank you*, puts food on his family's table by selling bootleg cd's and dvd's.

Rebecca whose checkered past scares companies into saying, *no thank you*, puts clothes on her children by escorting men.

Terrance whose checkered past scares companies into saying, *no thank you*, brings joy to his home by bearing flowers and candy. He tells his wife he found work making deliveries. He leaves out the part about delivering cocaine.

Marcus whose checkered past scares companies into saying, *no thank you*, drives his grandma to a dialysis center every other day, dropping her off at 1:00 and picking her up at 3:00. In between, he delivers stolen cars to a chop shop.

Fernando, an illegal alien who works off the books at a clothing store, sends money to his family in Peru every week.

Sally, an accountant, brings smiles and hope to people on the brink of foreclosure and bankruptcy by embellishing tax returns.

Ronnie who occasionally smokes weed laced with PCP never misses a Sunday at church where he prays for the uplift of friends neighbors children and himself.

PORTRAITS

Life

feel the heaviness of the word
touch soft grass, tree trunks and baby's bottoms
taste buttered popcorn, baked bread and mint tea
wade into warm, blue ocean water
listen to symphonies of playful children, laughing and singing
witness beavers, black bears and bald eagles
smell morning mist, fresh air and clean laundry
remind yourself you only have one of them
try to relate to the thousands of people doing push-ups,
playing checkers and counting cracks in walls after being
falsely accused, wrongfully convicted and sentenced
to do life

Client #73's Lament

what I never wanted was to be looked down upon like toxic waste in a landfill or to be placed in a position where I had to prove my worth as a human. I never consented to feeling inferior about how good I looked or how smart I was. I always aimed for the blue of the sky so I could land on white clouds, but I was born black and poor to a drug-addicted mother and an absentee father. I was raised in a neighborhood where the most attractive personalities belonged to drug-dealers, gang leaders and pimps.

Not long ago I was mistaken for being a drug dealer. I had no witnesses to vouch for my story that I was merely walking home and my lawyer was unable to persuade the predominantly white jury that I didn't do it. Now I am home free after living behind bars for four years, but I am not really free because I still have a felony conviction on my record and nobody will hire me and I am barred from getting a license to start a business, and now the best work I can find is making seven-fifty an hour through a temp agency, and my baby's mama keeps nagging me for money, and my own family has disowned me, and all I want is a reliable job and some respect, and to know when it will all end, and how things can change, and what is my destiny.

Listening

my imagination cannot fly
in a vacuum

on the topic of history
testimony trumps what dreams can conjure

rape and robbery bear a family resemblance
to slavery and Nazi oppression

pain dressed in plainclothes is the first cousin
to pain dressed in drag

different histories prevent wet dreams
of a uniform culture

testimonies contain fruits and berries needed
to build bonds between north and south

cantaloupes and raspberries offer sweet juices,
common ground for breaking bread, sharing it

words between words contain tools for shrinking ignorance
together, we can slice supremacy down to the ground

Portrait of a Prosecutor

She refuses to walk the streets at lunchtime for fear of running into somebody who she has wrongfully jailed.

She prefers to deal with the accused as numbers on a piece of paper, or as "defendants" twenty feet away from her in shackles.

She refuses to speak with them off-of-the-record in a huddle with their attorneys, even when invited by those attorneys, for fear of developing messy sticky feelings.

She believes the police never tell lies and can be trusted with large sums of money when nobody is watching them.

She threatens alleged victims with jail if they fail to come to court, even when they are begging for the charges to be dropped.

She tells alleged victims exactly what to say before they testify.

She refuses to consider the damage prison will do to the ties that bind children and fathers, wives and husbands, mothers and sons.

She refuses to see them as her equals in this world, as humans.

She loves to keep them in jail until they have broken and turned into putty for her to play with.

Sometimes, she throws them a greasy bone,
but never a real meal to replenish them.

She triple-locks her door at home and sleeps alone.

At the Edge of an Abyss

at the holiday party, I mistook warm hugs
firm handshakes and cheek kisses
as signs that the war was over.
I thought they were confessing their sins
and repenting

the next time in court, thick black smoke grabbed my throat
as I realized I had been duped

the abyss is filled with red hot embers
the products of a world that fosters
pimps and prostitutes with judicial doctorate degrees

if I heard screeching and saw winged shadows growing smaller
and smaller,
vultures became memories

I saw raw flesh being picked clean by prosecutors who sent
innocent men away to live behind bars

ancient trees, vibrant with freshly grown green leaves,
sob with anguish as they witness pimps and prostitutes smiling at
the accused and then talking trash about them
behind their backs

here, on cracked earth from a drought, desperate for
moisture in the form of mercy,
I stand suffering with the accused as Christ did with sinners
wondering why no judge or prosecutor believes in
rehabilitating the broken

at night, I cast wide eyes towards thirsty skies,
wondering how anybody who bleeds like me could
steal all of the fresh water available for caged persons to drink
by removing all remaining hope for them to reunite with their
families

today's air is filled with a resounding chorus of *no's:*
no, your client may not get less time
no, he may not get probation
no, she may not get a drug program

this death chant makes crackling sounds
like blue flames cracking deep into the night
I stand as far away from the flames as a pitcher stands from a batter,
yet I feel the heat as if I stood right next lava, burning red

Strange Business

I want to retire from this business
the trips I take require travel to three distant lands
one where the dominant sound is the drum
one where the weather is usually cold
one where men wear long hats with feathers

some of my guests have pale faces and dog-like hair
others have full lips with cheeks ranging
        from an almond brown to a deep mahogany

at night I hear countless cries
who on earth is being attacked by piranhas?

during the day, I hear songs from different parts of me:
from my chest I hear songs that boast of sexual conquest
        and the claiming of foreign lands
from my bowels I hear chants and hymnals that speak
        of raising children, breaking bread and sharing

some of the voices are hoarse from screaming and weeping
others are polished from sipping fine wines coffees and teas

this business has made me suicidal
I search for ways to kill myself
to run aground or impale myself
anything to shut down shop

Shameless Sentence

Thirty years in the Department of Corrections! shouts the prosecutor,
unable to appreciate the full impact of the sentence
she is recommending

Joe has been convicted of kidnapping his own child from
his child's mother's home.
the child's mother lied on the witness stand when she was
asked if Joe had ever spent time with their child

the child will now grow up without a father
the father will now be deprived of school graduations,
all ceremonies celebrating marriage
and the birth of his grandchildren

have we no shame?
we who only see the crimes,
passing judgment on others,
without considering the motives,
without regarding the bigger picture

I Can't Resist

I can't resist the smell of fresh flowers in spring time,
the color of burnt orange on falling leaves
the flavor of pistachios
the sound of trumpets in a good jazz song
or the feel of a kitten's soft warm underbelly
these things send me to a place where I can forget about my
    clients going to prison for crimes they did not commit
to a place where my shoulders and back can finally relax
    because I am not worried about being yelled at by
        ego-driven judges
or patronized by self-righteous prosecutors who know
    nothing about surviving with little to no money or
        shelter or respect

Swimming Lessons

when I am inches from you or even several yards away,
my toes curl into knots, my heart beat nearly stops
and my thoughts do somersaults into a lake where spirits
of lovers from centuries past provide swimming lessons
for present-day Romeos.

if you can find a man who loves you more than me,
please let me meet him
so I can expose him for being a sham
and convince you:
there is no man who loves you more than me.

The Beauty of Trees

yesterday I saw
green trees
smiling
and I smiled back

they were smiling
like people
at peace
with the wind
that surrounds
in the spring
and the fall

or like stars
in the sky
and the beams
that fall down
from the moon
on cool nights
like this night

The Brightness of You

all last week,
I watered three plants which looked
tired and ready to quit
today,
they stand tall and proud
I told them about you

Dinner's Going To Be Cold

He can't wait to get home from work. He can't wait to see his kids whose laughter melts him, his dog whose paws and licks disarm him, and his NBA game on cable which thrills him. Most of all, he can't wait to eat a home cooked meal with his wife whose smile is shaped liked a swinging yo-yo and whose eyes gleam like the shine on a new car.

Two pale-skinned men dressed in blue with silver badges have different plans. They need to meet their quota for arrests for the day. It doesn't matter to them if no one actually committed a crime. Anyone fitting their criminal profile will suffice. Who better fits that profile than a dark skinned male driving with rap music booming from his car windows? Who better fits that profile than a man whose record reveals he once broke the law as a juvenile by "possessing a weapon for an unlawful purpose?" His rap sheet fails to explain that the so-called weapon was a pocket knife he took to his junior high school to show off to friends, but school officials mistakenly believed he was carrying it to threaten someone's life. As for his current alleged crime, the myth of selling a small bag filled with an unknown white substance to an unidentified buyer who the cops were unable to catch and arrest will be good enough to hold him for at least one night.

He won't get to see his wife, kids, dog or NBA game, or eat that home-cooked meal because none of those things are available at the place filled with steel bars and concrete blocks.

So-Called Predators

when Danny was thirteen he was curious about female anatomy. He dreamed about touching girls whose breasts were fully developed. One day, during a break in his eighth grade class, he squeezed the breasts of one of his female classmates. Some of the boys who watched him were impressed by his courage and cheered him on. The girl was horrified. She reported the incident to her parents who pressed criminal charges on her behalf against Danny for Criminal Sexual Contact. Danny was prosecuted and found to be guilty for an offense which did not carry any jail time but required him to register as sex offender for the rest of his life.

when Jamal was fifteen, he slapped a fifteen year old girl on her butt as a joke. The girl was not amused. She reported it to her parents who pressed criminal charges on her behalf against Jamal for Criminal Sexual Contact. Jamal was prosecuted and found to be guilty for an offense which did not carry any jail time but required him to register as sex offender for the rest of his life.

Marcus was 18 when he went to a local nightclub and began socializing with a girl who was fifteen. The girl looked to be at least 18 years old and she even told him she was 18. One thing led to another and Marcus ended up having consensual sex with her later that evening. The girl believed she had made a love connection, but when Marcus never called her back, she decided to get even by pressing charges against him for rape. Even though she later admitted to the police that she had consented, the sex was considered to be statutory rape because she was technically too young to consent. Marcus was prosecuted and convicted for the crime which did not carry any jail time but required him to register as sex offender for the rest of his life.

Her Smile

golden pastures
like swirling winds
float endlessly
toward kingdoms of
rich feelings
playfulness
like carousels
popsicles
in summertime

maybe if
she would just
smile again
all of the
magical
creatures would
twist and spin
shamelessly

on dark green
blades of love
to bright songs
from chirping
parakeets

Essence

the darkness of midnight of charcoal of shadows of ebony

the sweetness of mangoes of licorice of custard of sugar cane

the softness of rose petals of feathers of silk of newborn baby skin

the joyous sound of prayed-for rain of children's laughter of jazz

the fragrance of honeysuckle of morning dew of cinnamon

the promise of me of you of us of here of now

Michael

his lawyer did a hellava job:
    he was a pit bull in the courtroom
    he took work home and worked on weekends
    he returned all of my phone calls
    he let me call him late at night to answer my questions
    he sent investigators to the scene of the alleged crime to
        take pictures
        measure distances
        look for witnesses

the judge tried to intimidate Michael into taking a plea:
    he yelled and screamed at him
    told him he would give him *life* if he lost
    acted like he was the king of the jungle

Michael resisted

I raced to the courtroom with our two children, dressed in my
    best floral blouse to impress the jury
I had rehearsed my testimony all night, eager to help Michael get out
so he could resume being the father he once was:
    helping me to pay rent
    taking our kids to school
    reminding them to pray five times a day

when the verdict came out, I grabbed their hands,
    anxious to end this sleepless chapter in our lives

It was not the end we prayed for

how could this happen?

my God!
          my God!
                    my God!

what will we do now?

If You Were A Leaf

if you were a leaf
I'd press you
frame you
save you
look at you daily
and kiss you
go back to your mother tree
and thank her
thank her for breeding you and feeding you
and then I would share you
share you by showing you off to neighbors
and even strangers
and by telling the world, *look at this leaf!*
look at this beautiful leaf!
it is a leaf that smells like a rose
feels like a feather
and shines like the color of gold
it is a friendly and caring leaf
it cannot make you sneeze
and it will not let you down
it'll make you smile in the morning
dance in the evening
and sing sweet songs
before you go
to sleep

Jeremy

Jeremy is laid off from work

he exhausts his unemployment benefits
he needs to do work on his house

he takes tools worth ten dollars from a store
the store staff tackles him
accuses him of shoplifting, a misdemeanor;
punishable with a fine and community service.
the prosecutor doesn't want him to get off easy
she changes the charge to robbery
and adds a bogus charge of resisting arrest.
both are felonies punishable with five to ten years of jail.
the prosecutor assumes the jury will find him guilty of something

six months in jail breaks Jeremy's spirit.
the prosecutor dangles a carrot called probation if
he pleads guilty to a felony charge normally
reserved for when the value of stolen goods is
more than five hundred dollars.
he pleads guilty to the trumped-up charge.

nobody wants to hire Jeremy for work.
the stigma of felony record is too much to overcome.
he can no longer apply for a license to start a business.
he can no longer apply for the armed services.
he can no longer get accepted into a college.
his life is destroyed.

Holding on versus Letting go

I want to let go when holding on
bites me like a mosquito
mocks me like a broken record
chases me like an angry shadow
sinks me like a broken plane
steals from me like wrinkles

I want to hold on when I see
flower buds breaking through skins and nails
or when I see random acts of kindness like
there is a piece of lint in your hair;
please let me remove it
or whenever I receive
any unexpected compliment
and the only desired return
is a smile
shining bright
like fresh popcorn

From Bridges to Ashes

after she asked her mother, who was retired and in poor health, to come live with her so she could take care of her

after her mother helped raise her two kids for the next five years by driving them to and from school, babysitting them and tutoring them while she travelled to London Paris and Florence, and went on numerous dates with men she met on the internet

after she used the money her mother made from selling the only house she owned to build a swimming pool and expand her house so it would be suitable for her and her children to live comfortably

after she used her mother to buy her a new car new furniture new windows for the whole house, a new washing machine drying machine dishwasher and a new paint job for both inside and outside the house, exhausting her mother's life savings

and after she never thanked her mother for doing anything

after all of this, she calls her mother a bad parent, kicks her out of the house, forbids her from taking any of the furniture, screams at her as if she were a child, calls the cops on her for trying to take the furniture, fabricates charges against her for threatening her life with a knife, allows them to drag her off in handcuffs like a common thug, never calls any family member or family friend to try to diffuse the situation before calling the cops, never calls her only brother to apprise him of anything, choosing instead to call a distant cousin who then calls her brother who has to leave work and drive four hours to try in vain to bail mom out of jail before she has to spend the night on blood-stained mattresses smelling of piss, never asks the prosecutor to dismiss the charges, traumatizes her mother for over two months with the possibility of a ten year prison sentence, never calls her only brother to discuss anything, and gloats in court when their mother, in a move made purely to "get it over with" and avoid worrying about what would happen if a judge or a jury disbelieved her version of what happened, pleads guilty to a crime which she did not commit

after all of this, bridges became smoldering ashes.

One Thing that Clarifies My Life

this sound this call this response
this symphony in the form of whistling trees,
eastward winds and threatening storms
this strange hiss emanating from dark woods,
burrowing through moonbeams
this echo from locusts crickets owls wolves bats and coyotes
this orchestra from creatures far and near,
dark and light, tall and small, black and white
this rich sound which sweetens the air and soothes me
how sweet this sound
how sweet this sound
how sweet

Even Now

as the rain falls and sleep is calling me, I hunger
for the way your cool lips on my skin leave
blueprints to paradise

for the way your raspy voice in my ear
makes hairs on my legs jump
like jack rabbits

for the way in which you say my name
casts sun rays and moonbeams throughout
the valley of my life and dreams

for the way your bold eyes alone
can call my bluff and freeze me
if I ever threaten to leave

for the way your soft touch triggers shock waves
changing fantasies into facts and
black holes into bright stars

Tyrone

my husband Tyrone has a brother named Willie

we always knew Willie used drugs and occasionally sold
them to support his own drug habit, but we had no idea
he was a major dealer

one weekend, Willie asked Tyrone to housesit for him
Willie said he needed to leave town to attend business.
he gave Tyrone a key chain with several keys on it
but except for the front door key, he never
explained what each key was for,

Tyrone jumped at the opportunity because
Willie had satellite TV which allowed Tyrone to lose himself
for several hours watching basketball and football
games that the main networks never showed

Tyrone had no warning when the cops came crashing into
Willie's apartment, flashing a search warrant.
one of the keys opened a closet containing
several kilos of cocaine along with sawed off shot gun
and several scales for weighing and dividing the drugs

Tyrone tried to explain that he knew nothing
but they charged him with running a drug manufacturing ring –
– a charge which normally carries ten to twenty years in prison
but because Tyrone has old convictions from his younger days,
he could get life in prison

for the last three years, Tyrone has been waiting for trial
his bail is too high for anyone we know to spring him
I now raise our three children by myself with the help of welfare
my jail visits are limited to one day per month
we lost our house and our cars,
no one has heard from or seen Willie since Tyrone's arrest
Tyrone has no way of proving that he was not involved with Willie
his life is now in the hands of his attorney and God
life as we knew it is over

Shifting the Balance of Power

if police officers approach me, detain me with their hands,
and begin to attack me with questions,
I can reach into my own arsenal of questions to
cut off the attack:
Officer, do you mind if I record this conversation with my cell phone?
Officer, since you have touched me and restricted my freedom to flee,
do you know you have committed the crime of false imprisonment,
harassment and assault, for which I can now press charges against you?
Officer, since you have not accused me of a crime,
can you please tell me what gives you the right to interrogate me?
Officer, since you dare to continue with your conduct, may I please have your
full name, badge number and the name of your boss?
Officer, since you do not have an arrest warrant or a search warrant,
do you mind if I report your conduct to your boss
and your Office of Internal Affairs?
Officer, do you mind asking any of these questions to my attorney?

A Humbling Experience

I am the only one who visits him
family and friends have abandoned him
he is my approximate age and skin color
one or two bad choices in life are all that separate us
he beats me in chess most of the time
he grasps legal concepts as quick as a calculator
he finishes my sentences before I can get them out
I have no doubt he would have been
a better attorney than me
I am his link to the outside world
a relief from the horror of gang fights
cramped living space
putrid air
spoiled milk
and stale bread

Relieving the Moon

the moon is sick
its color resembles vomit
it no longer illuminates the night
it begs for vitamins and minerals in the form of
fewer SUV's and more green trees
blue birds and brown bats understand the moon
they sing and pray for its speedy recovery
the gods respond with hurricanes and tropical storms,
disabling the spoils of humans,
temporarily forcing a return to firelight, walking,
eye-to-eye contact and hand-written letters,
momentarily relieving the moon

I Stand Accused

I stand accused of failing to use
the best of my heart to make works of art
like sweet jazz
melting
into rich watercolors

my penalty is walking a plank
that hangs above a sea filled with
submarines and warships
instead of joyful creatures,
peaceful whales and starfish

I am further condemned to passing judgment
on those who do not fit the norm
instead of trying to understand them,
to love them

to escape
I must make friends with freedom
and uncertainty
they will empower me to cast new spells
bringing rainbows to renegades
stranded on the margins

The Forgotten People

the incarcerated are the forgotten people
the people the newspapers never report on
the people never discussed on talk radio
when was the last time you heard of
someone being raped or killed in prison?
the numbers might surprise you

the forgotten people have lives with wives, kids, jobs and dreams
they are people who bleed when they are beaten by police batons
and cry when they learn their kids have graduated from school

they are people hidden behind bullet proof glass,
metal bars and concrete blocks
people who got caught up with the wrong crowd
at the wrong time and place
some of them are completely innocent
they were just standing near or walking past the real criminals
guilt by association is not supposed to be the law of the land
but it is
similar hair texture, skin color and clothes should not be factors
but they are

Manic Lover

There once was a man named Manic Lover who loved Mystery like there was no tomorrow. A car accident took Mystery away. He tried to fill the void by seeking out string-free forms of romance with strangers but he always got strung-out and felt cold. These pursuits soured him on the idea that he could ever fall in love again. He denied the itchy-scratchy feelings that he felt in his palms and his chest when he later met Jazz Lover - a caramel-tinted woman who could change the direction of winds with a blink of her eyes. He denied that those feelings could be seeds to new beginnings and fresh fruits.

Two other women named Reggae and Hip Hop begged Manic to dance in the rain and play in the snow, but Manic refused. Reggae and Hip Hop made sketches larger than life in the air with their dance moves and they became carefree children in love with life with their games in the snow. The rain would have taught Manic that he had nothing to lose by believing that his bond with Mystery could be matched or surpassed by a bond with another woman. The snow would have taught him that pearl-white joy was promised if he would just laugh at himself and look forward to dreams and do all that he could to make them come true.

ANN DARROW AND KING KONG

(inspired by the 2005 version of *King Kong*)

i.

I touched his nose
I stroked his arms
I brought music into his life
I danced for him
I laughed for him
I screamed for him
I taught him to respect the words *yes* and *no*
I inspired him to climb tall buildings
I tried to protect him
I cried for him

ii.

I held her tight to my chest
I tickled her with my heartbeat
I taught her to ignore the words *beast* and *thing*
I made her fly like a flamingo
I made her feel like the greatest woman in the world
I beat my chest and roared for her
I busted my chains for her
I ice-skated for her
I caught her when she fell
I died for her

Portrait of Him

i.

boy gives girl
small wrapped gift
girl thinks gift
small pretty ring
girl opens gift
finds small clown
girl hates gift
calls boy nerd

girl don't see
boy meant well
girl can't see
boy likes girl
girl won't see
clown just joke
girl fails see
love
            has
no
            rules

ii.

he circles the moon in the night with his
vision of children flying on carpets
searching for playthings and lost pets

by day he stands upright
making funny shapes out of clouds
in an effort to repair the damage done

by broken promises and people
who insist he has an ulterior motive for
telling them they are beautiful

he dreams of white sand and running on it
          with or without her
of dancing to slow jams and funk
          with or without her
of catching the bright yellow flower called the sun
                    rising and blooming in the morning
with or without her

he makes angels in the snow
he twinkles when he smiles
he has cried during movies
he exchanges ideas about music and dance
          before he exchanges bodily fluids
his rap is clumsy

How He Lives

with eyes towards large pictures
by laughing at himself

with jazz, rap and reggae
by setting goals and fighting for them

with full-bodied wine and extra sharp cheddar
by making friends with spiders

with streaks of lightening
by floating on sea water

with travelocity.com
by dancing until sweat drips

with hammer and nail
by swimming with sea turtles

with pralines and cream
by gulping on fresh air while pondering green pastures

with one foot in history, the other foot forward
by getting his hands dirty with red earth and shovels

with milkshakes and waffle cones
by standing clear of Hollywood lies about the real world

with red bricks and mortar
by not caring what others think

with groundnut soup and rice fufu
by giving thanks for each day, twice a day

Clenched Fist

I saw Ben's clenched fist out of the corner of my eyes
the judge had just finished telling him he was released.
minutes before, Ben pled guilty to burglary – a crime
he did not commit, but pleading guilty was the only way to
escape the mice-infested, cold-water only, no-heat-in the-winter,
no cold-air-in-the-summer, fighting-everyday,
God-forsaken place called the County Jail
his ex-girlfriend had falsely accused him of breaking and entering
her home with the intent to commit a crime
the home was actually in his name
but law in his State says that once a woman who has been living
with a man alleges domestic violence,
the man can be forced to live on the streets, homeless.
on the day of the alleged crime, Ben was trying to get his clothes.
the door was unlocked but the law calls it a "breaking" when
a person is not invited in
startled by his appearance, she screamed and called the cops
he was gone before they arrived
she made up a story about him pushing her to the floor and
threatening to harm her
after being arrested and jailed, Ben insisted on going to trial.
it would be his word against hers
judges and juries typically believe "her,"
and the penalty if he lost would be up to five years in prison,
but he was adamant,
unable to afford bail and the judge refused to lower it
a year in a jail can do terrible things to people
the false allegations never fazed Ben
but jail destroyed him
after a year, he begged me: *Please, I'll do anything to get out of here.*

Beauty in Nonsense

he has discussions with dogwood trees sunflowers and horses

he daydreams about children sailing the seas
on the backs of silvery gray dolphins, sharing
ghost stories passed down while eating
roasted marshmallows

he finds beauty in those who others call ugly stupid or weird

he enjoys music sung in foreign tongues -
- Ethiopian, Portuguese, Congolese and French-Creole

he blesses black white yellow brown and red people
even when they don't see him and
not just after they have sneezed

women have cheated and lied on him,
yet he still believes soft bright flowers grow inside
of each one he meets

he sees nothing wrong with believing that
this could be his second or third
but not his last life

he finds it perfectly plausible that his next life could be as
a poodle, a pelican or a pear tree

he doesn't make sense
there is beauty in nonsense

Drug Dealer's Anthem

*Come, brother, come. Let's lift it.**
we don't want to become a statistic.
it's not our fault we can't find real jobs.
too many factories are run by snobs.
we are young, gifted and black,
but broke as hound dogs

black bodies are easily scarred
nobody likes the attention from scars
come brother, come;
help us to become stars

customers far and near can't wait to get high
real jobs in this economy are hard to come by
welfare checks and food stamps only go so far,
but we can do this work from the trunk of a car

sell, sell, sell, but don't get caught
it's as easy as making a bank shot
everybody wants to make an honest buck
but with our rap sheets, we don't give a fuck

black bodies are easily scarred
nobody likes the attention from scars
come brother, come;
help us to become stars

*This first line is borrowed from the poem "Cotton Song" by Jean Toomer.

Her Hands

he has studied her hands
as they helped her to tell stories
fingers and palms fully extended and gesticulating
and he has touched them

their smooth texture reminds him of emeralds
the warm flesh of them begets images of peace:
        a quiet lake
                a cloudless sky
        orange sunflowers
                blue butterflies

the Taj Mahal is one of the wonders of the world.
he asks her, *will you go with me to see it?*
he yearns to watch her when her eyes behold a treasure
just like her hands

Pre-Trial Hearing

he pleads not guilty
smart man
he is remembering something about the right to a fair trial
and to the presumption of innocence

he is resisting the pressure
from the prosecutor, the media,
the alleged victim's family
newspapers and television
to plead guilty to an offense
which he did not commit

he knows there is a ground higher than the sewage gutters
where cops find refuge
he is motivated by every image of strange fruit
hanging from trees from his ancestor's past

poor audience
they believe this courtroom scene
is a rerun of television legal dramas where
the prosecutor is always portrayed as the underdog
and the person accused stands a better-than-even chance
of walking free

they are oblivious to the reality of cops manufacturing
evidence and reports in order to hide beatings inflicted
upon the accused and to force them to confess
and the reality of prosecutors overcharging people
to fool juries into believing that with so many crimes charged,
the accused must be guilty of something

missing from the court room drama is an indictment
of the cops who beat down the helpless civilian
and then helped themselves to the contents of his wallet
with shameless smiles on their faces

Johnny

Johnny lives near the intersection of Rosa Parks Boulevard and Martin Luther King Street in Paterson, New Jersey. His neighborhood is falling apart. Gangs have taken over the cocaine market in the neighborhood and countless houses are boarded up. Johnny has never been in trouble with the law. He enjoys basketball and hip hop music. In his spare time, he likes to freestyle rap with his high school buddies. One summer evening, Johnny is battle rapping with kids on a street corner. A small crowd has gathered to listen. Out of nowhere, sirens suddenly crash the gathering, bullhorns are blown, and blinking red lights decorate the street. Some boys run and get away. Others are thrown to the ground and threatened. The cops beat several boys with their batons even after the boys are handcuffed and on the ground. Fast forward to closing arguments at the trial. The prosecutor is dramatizing the event, parading around the well of the courtroom, emulating the act of selling vials of cocaine on a street corner, shouting *This man conspired to sell drugs with his buddies because the police saw him with his buddies who were seen selling drugs.* The overconfident prosecutor, with blind faith in his guilt, smiles while pointing her finger at Johnny who sits in the Defendant's chair. Johnny now raps in prison where he must live for the next ten years.

Snow on a Convent's Lawn

Snow on a convent's lawn conjures images of innocence and
peace, but inside the convent, not more than ten feet away is
a group of writers from diverse backgrounds who have rented
out the building, where conservative nuns live, to write
poems about war, wild sex and divorce, or about how they
dream about getting laid or getting blow jobs and drinking
vodka, or about how they struggle with drug addiction and
sex addiction, or about how they no longer believe in god
because of all their friends and family members who died too
young, tragically and painfully, or about how most Christian
faiths are too narrow to accommodate their beliefs in
reincarnation, the spirituality of animals plants and trees and
the virtues of premarital sex, or about how women robbed of
their virginity by stepfathers who could not control
themselves would love to have been nuns but can't, or about
how persons falsely accused and rotting away in prisons
would love to know how a convent hidden away in the
backwoods of New Jersey is relevant to their everyday lives.

LETTERS

Dear Lady Justice,

Are you the goddess of justice I seek? The goddess I seek is a soul sista' with a natural hairstyle. She carries a gun instead of an outdated sword, she wears an ankle bracelet to remind her she came from cotton fields instead of wine cellars, and she marches and protests with the masses instead of standing on the sidelines with clean hands. She immerses herself in the community, allows herself to be judged by those who she judges, and suffers with those who fight for greater freedom and dignity. She does not leave us alone in our agonies and struggles, but seeks us out in the ghettos, barrios, jails and prisons, and suffers with us.

Some say she should be blindfolded, but I know justice is not blind. Just as cops are not blind when they profile people based on race and ethnicity, she cannot save wrongly accused African Americans, Latinos and Muslims from the stinging whip of the law with covered eyes. There is no time or place for neutrality. Being able to identify victims of justice enables her to identify with them and serve them.

If you are the real goddess of justice, where were you when we needed you the most: laying in our own shit on slave ships, being sold like hogs on auction blocks, dangling like strange fruit from southern trees, being hosed down by the police, being bitten by police dogs, and being profiled, harassed and sometimes brutally beaten by the police even after Obama was elected?

We who serve and are served by the real goddess are pieces of glass, just like her, shattered by a mentality that encourages us to erect barriers between and among us, instead of reaching out to help each other solve common problems, overcoming common fears. Can your set of scales handle the weight of our problems?

Dear President Obama,

As a black man in America, I am proud to know you are the President of our country. Growing up, I experienced a lot of hatred from white folks who always assumed they were smarter, better looking and morally superior to me due to the color of their skin, the texture of their hair, the shape of their noses and the size of their lips. My physical appearance was always the butt of jokes told by white classmates, and white teachers always encouraged me to pursue either the army or a trade school, while they encouraged white students to pursue four year colleges. Because of the way they treated me, I developed an inferiority complex and I never thought I measured up. If you had been president when I was growing up, I would have had the psychological fortitude to withstand those white supremacist behaviors, but even your presidency back then might not have saved me from what happened to me later.

I am currently serving life in prison for a crime I did not commit. An all-white jury found me guilty of raping a white woman. The only evidence they had against me was the testimony of the alleged victim who told the police I was the perpetrator, even though she did not get a good look at the real perpetrator's face and there was no DNA evidence to back up her claim. She was mistaken, but it was my word against hers, and the all-white jury believed her. I will never spend time with my wife and children again.

In spite of my troubles, I still smile when I think of you and your wife and what you have done. By breaking the glass ceiling on what blacks can achieve and what people in charge should look like in this country, you have set the ball in motion to help eliminate the circumstances that caused me and thousands of others like me to be incarcerated.

Yours truly,

An Unlucky Black Man

Dear Members of the Jury,

I might get in trouble for passing you this note, but I believe it is important for you to know the truth:

the truth about how every cop who testified at trial has been reported to internal affairs for falsifying evidence, using excessive force during arrests and stealing money during strip searches

the truth about how cops are often motivated to press charges against people because they receive overtime pay for testifying in court

the truth about how prosecutors often tack on additional charges that they cannot prove in order to trick you into thinking that with all of the charges, the accused must be guilty of "something"

the truth about how seemingly small charges like trespassing, possession of small amounts of drugs and resisting arrest can sometimes send people to prison for decades

the truth about how you as a jury have the right to make a statement to society about what you think of police practices by ignoring the law and finding the accused NOT GUILTY of all charges

the truth about how I wish I could tell you all of this face-to-face, but if I did, I would be crucified.

Yours truly,

Attorney for the Accused

Dear Innocence Project,*

thank you for saving hundreds of black white and polka dot lives,
giving hope to countless more

thank you for making thousands of prosecutors look more stupid
than Homer Simpson

thank you for changing public opinion about the
reliability of eyewitness identifications

thank you for exposing the reality of false confessions

thank you for exposing fabricated scientific test results that have
led to wrongful convictions

thank you for helping numerous states to pass laws,
mandating the preservation of DNA evidence

thank you for inspiring freedom fighters in the fields of
law, science, philanthropy and grassroots politics

thank you for shaking us awake in the morning,
reminding us, *we still have work to do*

*For more information, visit www.innocenceproject.org.

REVELATIONS

Revelations

the dead have hired me to pass on messages to the living.
payment for my services will be the right to glimpse
at my own future, complete with color and sound,
or to chose my own reincarnated body,
human or otherwise,
complete with memory and wisdom

recent channelings I have performed include
telling a teenage boy his deceased father
    whom he never met
    died from the very cigarettes he would like to try,
telling a widower her husband cannot rest in peace
    until she tells their grown daughter that
    her real father is somebody else,
and telling a family of mourners that their loved one's death
    was not accidental or natural
    but deliberately caused
    by a secret lover

The Earth had Wanted Us All to Herself

She had wanted us all to herself but we were not satisfied with fresh fruits, vegetables, red soil and clear waters, placing our faith instead in our ability to steal, enslave, displace, rape and create artificial boundaries between black and white, civilized and savage, making love and praising God, choosing instead to befriend pesticides on plants, growth hormones for animals and weapons of mass destruction.

It was not always like this.

when everything we were, made and discarded was biodegradable, She could not get enough of us; She hungered for our feces and thirsted for our urine; campfires and songs sung around them entertained and warmed her; drum beats and dance steps massaged her back neck and legs; she grew flowers in pinks and purples to decorate hills and valleys, providing nectar for bees birds and butterflies and eye candy for the rest of us.

fistfights over women, even those bringing death, were acceptable because no air land or water was poisoned and new bodies were destined to be born again; She cringed when a-bombs struck cities in Japan, napalm purged villages in Vietnam, oil tankers spilled poison into her seas and burning fossil fuels began threatening all known life; She designed hurricanes tornadoes and earthquakes to keep us humble, but her efforts failed when we began to love flat screen TV's more than old-growth green trees.

She had wanted us all to herself
but we belittled her
and we betrayed her

Dancing Homo Sapiens

we danced into this world.
we shook and spun
and dipped and grooved
to natural rhythms
moans and groans of lovers who sweated for us,
footsteps and heartbeats of women who carried us,
raindrops singing birds chirping crickets and barking dogs.
we laughed and cried tears of joy for most of the trip.
by the time we arrived
we already knew our bodies:
how they responded to stress
and how they adored new rhythms
like new records being changed or scratched
by DJ's reading the pulse of a crowd.
we were nuclear power generators
yearning to power man-made constellations and comets.
we praised god with our dance moves
and brought heaven to earth with intensity.
dancing was our business
and we were ready to conquer the world.

My Worst Habit

(inspired by Frido Kahlo's "Broken Column")

my worst habit is my fear
that the world does not need a female Christ
that I have made the wrong choice
that I am just reinventing the wheel
  when the wheel is already well-built
that I have overestimated the value of sacrifice
  because nobody gives a damn
  and I cannot really save anyone
that my naked body, blood and tears will be wasted
that I will be misunderstood
that I will not measure up
that my grace is not sufficient
that my children will have no one to turn to for advice,
  for strength, for a shoulder to lean on,
  for someone who will not judge them
and that my people's history will repeat itself:
  we will be raped again
  our horses and buffaloes will be slaughtered again
  our corn and squash will be stolen again
  and our burial grounds will be bulldozed
    for development and redevelopment
again
  and again
    and again

There is Nothing Black or White

the cat meows, rubbing up against my leg with her arched back
posturing for me to feed her another can of turkey and giblets
   – the third one in the same day

I sit with book in hand –
   – a collection of short stories by Sherman Alexie
occasionally my mind drifts to questions such as, what if I
were born Native American and raised on a reservation?
how much different would I be, if at all?

Friday approaches and I don't have a date lined up
the last few women I took out are too fickle to ask out again
   their minds change with the direction of winds
some can't decide if they want me as a friend
or as more
or if my intentions are good
or suspicious
others carry too much baggage from previous men
   babies and babies' daddy drama,
   a view of life where everybody is out to get them,
   and vaginal walls that have been so elasticized,
   they cease to provide friction for new lovers

would a wife and children make me happy or more stressed?
would I feel more complete or just confined?
would I delight in the privilege of having an exclusive lover,
or would I get tired of the same pussy?

does everything have to be learned by way of trial and error,
or can we learn by listening to elders and even peers?

do we need to try crack-cocaine?

I wish I had a lighter set of concerns such as instructing
a friend on how to satisfy his girlfriend
instead, I lose sleep over how I'm going to win a trial where
my client is facing life if he loses, and the evidence against
him seems to be overwhelming,
yet I keep having nagging doubts about the official story:
statements by witnesses do not match
and there is an alternative explanation for what actually happened
there is nothing black or white about either guilt or innocence

sometimes I wonder if everything in life is just an illusion,
then I visit my clients in jail and the metal, unbreakable bars
crash me back to earth

death was invented to give tired souls a brief rest
before re-entering the world as new life-forms
in my next life, I'd like to be a duck

Squeeze It

squeeze it out of I-just-quit-my-job
        I-just-got-fired
        and I-can't-pay-my-rent
squeeze it out of credit card debt
        mortgage debt
        and student loan debt
squeeze it out of being rejected from a job
        and rejected by a love interest
squeeze it out of being passed up by cab drivers
        and followed in stores by security guards

squeeze it
squeeze it

squeeze it out of growing up with missing-in-action fathers
        and growing up with drug-addicted mothers
squeeze it out of judges who did not care
        and social workers who did not care
squeeze it out of living on blocks decorated by
        junkies prostitutes and panhandlers
squeeze it out of being beaten down by cops
        and lied about by cops
squeeze it out of sleeping in our own excrement in
        the bowls of ships for weeks
squeeze it out of picking cotton and picking sugar cane for free
squeeze it out of a history of not being considered fully human
        and not being taken seriously

squeeze it
squeeze it

squeeze it into double-dutch dance moves
squeeze it into basketball cross-over moves
squeeze it into poetry paintings and sculptures, transforming lives
squeeze it into hip-hop sweet jazz gut-bucket blues and funky R&B,
        making folks move their feet and nod their heads
squeeze it into testimonies about beating impossible odds
        like President Obama and Nelson Mandela

squeeze it
squeeze it
squeeze it

squeeze your soul
squeeze your soul
squeeze your soul

squeeze it into soul juice
squeeze it into soul juice
squeeze it into soul juice

Why Innocent People Plead Guilty

Jesse is temporarily free because he made bail after being falsely accused of trespassing. He wanted a trial but he pled guilty because he lacked a witness to vouch for his story and chances were high that a judge or a jury would believe the police version over his. He pled guilty because he lacked the patience to wait up to two years for a trial, or the vacation time to keep taking off from work for court appearances where judges and prosecutors look at him like dirt, or the connections to anybody who helped give those people their jobs, to make the charges disappear. He pled guilty because the penalty for pleading guilty was probation and a fine plus the stain of a criminal record, but no prison time which would have been certain if he lost trial. He pled guilty because it freed him from the nightmare of being removed from his wife and children for an indefinite amount of time.

Jessica has languished in jail for a year because she could not afford bail after being falsely accused of selling cocaine. She wanted a trial but she pled guilty because she lacked a witness to vouch for her story and chances were high that a judge or a jury would believe the police version over hers. She pled guilty because she lacked the patience to wait up to two years for a trial, or the energy to be constantly frowned upon by judges and prosecutors who look at her like dirt, or the connections to anybody who helped give those people their jobs, to make the charges disappear. She pled guilty because the penalty for pleading guilty was probation and a fine plus the stain of a criminal record, but not five to ten years of prison if she had lost trial. She pled guilty because it freed her from jail and gave her the chance to fight for her kids who were taken by social services based on these charges.

Harold's Calling

Harold is a court-appointed defense attorney who would like to
ruin the Hollywood image of what he does

he never defends criminals
he defends persons accused of committing crimes

he is not a "public pretender" - someone who pretends to be
a friend of the accused just to get them to plead guilty

he makes less money than most truck drivers, trash collectors
and plumbers, but he does it because he loves it

he almost never lets his clients spill their guts to prosecutors,
choosing instead to keep his cards tight to his vest and
play smart poker by poking holes into the evidence

he has never defended a serial rapist or serial killer
most of his clients are young men accused of selling
very small quantities of drugs

he often visits the jail to interview clients
the experience never frightens him
he feels humbled and privileged to go

he never regrets defending people when he knows they
are probably guilty
everyone deserves a fair trial
and it is the prosecutor's job to prove guilt
beyond a reasonable doubt

What I Didn't Expect

what I didn't expect when I started this work was how much like me my clients and I would be in our age height skin color eye color hair style and background, how so many of them like to read or listen to poetry and how well some of them write it, how so many of them bury themselves in the law library at the jail to the point where they can articulate the law just as well if not better than me, how difficult it is to establish trust between them and me, how debilitating the perception of public defenders as those who merely pretend to be your friend so they can sell you out to the prosecutors, how grateful inmates can be for visiting them because no one else either wants to visit them or is allowed to visit them because people with criminal records are not allowed to visit them, how much like apes in zoos my clients seem when they are crowded into holding cells, how much more I enjoy visiting a jail instead of pushing papers behind a desk because the visits keep me grounded and connected to real people with real problems, how flirtatious my female clients would be with me, how much the spirits of my clients would be broken by the police prosecutors and judges who looked down upon them to the point where I had to give motivational talks before or after I discussed their legal case with them, how much I would have to pay attention to my own body posture and state of mind in public because now I had an image in the community connected to my work, how self-righteous and heartless so many of the prosecutors could be when recommending long prison sentences, how easily juries from the suburbs trust police officers, and how I didn't expect that after years and years of doing this work I would continue to be surprised.

PRAYERS

I Am Looking For a Jury

I am looking for a jury that believes all people are created equal

for a jury that can honestly presume someone to be innocent
before any purported proofs of guilt are presented

for a jury that will not be fooled by phrases such as *Isn't it strange that this happened or that happened* because they know that strange occurrences are not the same as proof beyond a reasonable doubt

for a jury that will not give more weight to the testimony of a
police officer than the testimony of a non-police officer

for a jury that will not rush to judgment because the court day is
almost over and they don't want to come back another day and
the easy way out is to find him or her guilty

for a jury that has individuals confident enough to say *I don't care what the rest of you believe, I believe he is innocent*

for a jury that will not be a rubber stamp for the prosecutor's so-called official version of what happened

for a jury that understands that cops sometimes make up stories
to protect themselves

for a jury that sincerely believes that people can be rehabilitated,
therefore, one or two prior convictions does not necessarily mean
that the accused person is guilty of the present allegations

for a jury that will not expect the accused person to prove his or her innocence because they know that the prosecutor has the burden of proof at all times and it never shifts to the defendant

for a jury that understands that sometimes innocent people are manipulated and tricked into making confessions after being starved for 12 hours, yelled at for 12 hours, and told that they will be released if they just admit to the charge

for a jury that knows that hundreds and hundreds of people who were wrongly convicted have been exonerated by DNA evidence

I am looking for a jury

I Am Looking For a Judge

I am looking for a judge who believes that making people watch the film *It's a Wonderful Life* five times can be a viable alternative to sending them to prison

for a judge who has the guts to dismiss any case that stinks of ethnic or racial profiling

for a judge who admits when he or she is wrong and apologizes on-the-record in front of a court full of people

for a judge who is willing to personally visit the scene of an alleged crime to see if the police surveillance point was not fabricated

for a judge who believes the man who insists he only confessed because the cops starved, beat and threatened him

for a judge who believes the woman who says she only agreed to let the cops search her house without a search warrant because they said they would take her kids away and put her in jail if she didn't sign a "consent to search" form

for a judge who is not scared to rule against the prosecutors, refusing to be their rubber stamp

for a judge who cares enough to give someone another chance at probation because he understands that relapse is a natural part of recovery

for a judge who sees the potential Barack and Michelle
Obama in some of my clients

I am looking for that judge

In Search of Beautiful

mayday! mayday!
beautiful is missing!

please help us to find her.
here are some clues you can use:

black birds talking about the journey
of flying south and then flying back north

red oak trees talking about the experience
of shedding leaves and then growing them back

gargoyles singing good time music by
Al Green and Aretha Franklin

crowded streets and street lights,
guiding people to a place called peace

chimpanzees throwing a banana and ice cream party
with people invited

butterflies congregating on mountaintops,
protesting pesticides

pimps and prostitutes in the business
of selling lemonade and chocolate cookies

gangsters giving up gangbanging to read
bedtime stories to the bedridden

pushers pushing pencils for people
to sketch starfish and sunflowers

more people caring enough to say, *here is my hand!*
don't let go! I've got you.

It is Time

I imagine myself lost
in a series of nightmares
with no one to wake me up
and carry me to a place
where I can work without
monsters staring over my back,
threatening to report me to
thought police

it is time to knock on doors
wake up naive lovers blinded by flesh
and tell them, *the circle*
has been broken
and must be rebuilt

the materials needed do not include reality TV
fast food fries or even sunglasses
only a willingness to listen to victims
of abuse and neglect
and bear witness for them

other useful materials might include
a burning branch from a campfire
to help navigate whatever traces of sanity
that enemies of self-determination
have not stamped out of me

finally, a hole-puncher
not to punch random holes in the sky
but to round off the holes already made

by bulldozers and bazookas
so we can fill them
with laughter
and song

Freeze Frame

freeze frame the magic of the dance
if you will, I will dance with you forever

freeze frame the image of dreamers wading in water
if you will, I will run with you on the beach
until our bodies grow weary of running
on dreams

freeze frame the feeling of dreams coming true
if you will, I will bring you a fistful of flowers
flowers freshly picked from the garden
of freedom

freeze frame the feeling of freedom
freedom from arrows of sorrow that threaten to damage happiness
if you will, I will try to make your dreams come true

freeze frame the belief in answered prayers
prayers that ask for strength and wisdom
prayers that ask for courage and grace

if you will, I will pray with you
and ask for frozen frames
of happiness

I Want To Find That Woman

somehow somewhere someway
perhaps in another reincarnation
I want to find that woman who I met
        last week last month last year
that's right - all of those women
the ones who
        thrilled me when I first met them
        gave me goose bumps when I gazed into their eyes
        danced with me until my legs grew tired
        uttered thank you when I bought them a drink
        shattered my mind by responding to my advances
                with their undivided attention
        flattered me by telling me that I was different from
                all of the rest
yes, I want to find that woman
                find that woman
                find that woman
and thank her
        for giving me
the wrong number

Angel of War

last night, I heard the cries of a hundred babies
as they begged for their mothers whose
breasts had been chopped off

the night before, I smelled
the occupiers of my land
as they pissed and defecated
on my front porch
steps and lawn

today, I witnessed full grown men
dripping in sweat and weeping
as they ran for cover
from metallic rain

every day, I see green-helicoptered cannons
flying overhead
even though I never asked for protection
and never said I was scared

tonight, I am cooking a stew
of bullets and uranium
I plan to overcook it
to boil it down to nothing

what will your followers
fight with
then?

Made in the USA
Charleston, SC
26 January 2011